*The steps of a good man
are ordered by the Lord,
and He delights in
the details of his life.*

PSALM 37:23 (Doug Clay's paraphrase)

SPECIAL THANKS

to Mark Forrester, Communications; Julie Horner and Tammy Bledsoe, AG Publishing; Gregory Rohm, design; Paul W. Smith and Donna Swinford, editing; Rebekah Clute and team, Spanish editing; Greg Brown and our friends in the plant; and others at the national office who will be involved in distribution.

— **Doug and Randy**

ORDERED STEPS

introducing
DOUG CLAY
General Superintendent
Assemblies of God

RANDY HURST

ORDERED STEPS

02-4232

20 19 18 17 · 1 2 3 4

Printed in the United States of America

CONTENTS

PASSING THE TORCH

Doug Clay, is the first PK (preacher's kid) general superintendent to be raised by a single mother—his pastor-father had died suddenly of a heart attack when Doug was a young boy. Doug experienced a loving Assemblies of God church that surrounded him and his family. In his own words, he talks about the many spiritual dads in the church who made such a huge impact on his life. So in his growing up years, he was raised in a healthy church where he experienced the call of God for a full-time ministry journey. He followed that call to prepare for ministry at Central Bible College.

I first became aware of Doug Clay when he served as our national youth director. His leadership and influence were felt throughout the Fellowship. From there, he pastored a church in Ohio that had experienced three successive tragedies, in the way previous pastors had left. God, through Doug, brought a distraught church back to health and confidence. And it continues to be a life-giving church to this day. The Ohio District then elected Doug as district superintendent.

When I encountered a vacancy in the office of general treasurer, I had one name in mind—Doug Clay. I asked him if he would permit me to nominate him for that position. He agreed and the Executive Presbytery unanimously approved him. My rationale for selecting Doug to that position was simple—I always ask a specific first question when hiring or appointing others to office: "Is this the kind of person I would like other people to become like?" Doug absolutely fit that qualification. I asked him to serve, not simply because of his financial acumen, which he has, but because of the Christlike quality of his life and his capacity to be a spiritual leader in our Movement.

I am delighted to pass the torch of leadership to a good friend who is eminently qualified to lead our Fellowship!

—**George O. Wood,** *General Superintendent of the*
Assemblies of God, 2007–2017

WHO IS DOUG CLAY?

This book will introduce you to Doug Clay—as his family and friends know him.

You will meet a leader who is certain of his belief in biblical truth and in the Holy Spirit's guidance and enablement—foundations with which he grew up and by which he continues to live.

Ordered Steps offers a revealing journey through the insights and perspectives of those who know Doug best. As well, Doug shares his spiritual priorities and passions in his own words.

Doug's experiences remind us God sovereignly works circumstances for good in and through our lives. Tragedy in childhood, the spiritual strength of his family, and the nurturing care of his home church all worked together to bring Doug through extraordinary challenges early in life. Doug Clay's story is a telling illustration of the inspiring truth of divine providence—that God delights in the details of our lives, when we choose to let Him order our steps.

I first met Doug more than twenty years ago. He reached out to me in friendship and has encouraged me ever since. It has been a joy and privilege to travel in ministry together and just to spend time with him. My experience has mirrored those of his family and other friends, as I discovered when interviewing them for this book. Doug extends himself to people, affirming and motivating them, doing whatever he can to help others succeed in their journey with and service for the Lord.

As you read the perspectives of those I interviewed, one fact is clear—those who know him best respect him most.

—**Randy Hurst,** *AG World Missions Advancement director*

SECTION 1

FAMILY
LIFE

ORDERED STEPS

The drama of the *Titanic* still fascinates.

Almost a century ago, wealthy socialites and celebrities danced under the warm light of glittering chandeliers. Musicians played popular songs of the day, while the first-class passengers dined on delicacies. No one knew that in a few hours, the largest and most luxurious ocean liner ever built would sink beneath the waves. All the excited passengers who boarded the supposedly "unsinkable" ship for her maiden voyage would gladly have cancelled their trip, could they have foreseen the tragedy to come.

One of the scheduled passengers on the *Titanic* was J. Stuart Holden, the eloquent preacher of Saint Paul's Church in London. He had crossed the Atlantic many times to preach in the United States, often for the Bible conferences hosted by D. L. Moody. Less than twenty-four hours before the *Titanic* sailed, Holden's wife needed emergency surgery. The dilemma Holden faced was whether to fulfill his commitment to preach in the United States or to cancel his trip and remain with his wife. Trusting God's Word concerning his responsibility to his wife, he telegraphed the hosts of the conference that he would not be coming.

Holden's *Titanic* ticket hung framed on the study wall for the rest of his life as a testimony to God's faithfulness and guidance. J. Stuart Holden had twenty-two more years of influential ministry, including his leadership in the famous Keswick Convention where he introduced a strong missions emphasis, resulting in many missionaries reaching the lost around the world.

What would not have happened—what lives would not have been affected for Christ if Stuart Holden had chosen to make the voyage on the *Titanic*?

Less than a month after the *Titanic* sailed, a twenty-one-year-old young man left England for a new life in the United States. He had planned to travel on the *Titanic's* maiden voyage but changed his plans and took the next available ship a few weeks later—the SS *Grampian*—some of his descendants surmised because the fare was less. His choice to change ships would affect the future of countless lives.

Art Clay, Doug's father, with his father George

His name was George Edward Clay—grandfather of Doug Clay. Had George Clay not changed ships, Doug Clay would not have been born.

God's sovereignty and providence are magnificent mysteries. In Paul's letter to the Romans he says that God's ways are "unfathomable" (11:33, NASB) but also affirms that "God causes all things to work together for good." (8:28, NASB)

Many regretfully speculate about what *might* have happened in their lives if they had only made different choices. More importantly, what would *not* have happened in and through our lives if God hadn't acted in His providence?

To the surrendered follower of Christ, the dark clouds of regret concerning what might have been are dispelled by the shining light of

SS Grampian

what God causes to happen in our lives in spite of, and even through tragedy, sorrow, and pain.

After landing in Canada, George Clay traveled on an immigrant train to the United States, settling in Detroit. He sent for his fiancé, Martha, still in England to join him and they were married. George began working at the Solvay Chemical Processing Plant. A coworker, Arthur Shaw, who had also emigrated from England, began witnessing to him.

George and Martha's first child, their daughter Hazel, had several major medical problems. They had taken her to specialists but found no help. George told Arthur Shaw they would bring their daughter to a prayer meeting and, if she was healed, they would accept the Lord. She was healed, and George and Martha surrendered their lives to Jesus.

George and Martha began attending what were then called "cottage prayer meetings" in homes, where they began seeking the infilling of the Holy Spirit that they had heard about. Though he earnestly prayed to receive, George struggled and was discouraged. Because they were all from England, at the close of each meeting, they had tea and biscuits (cookies). One night George was asked to pray the blessing on their refreshments. As he began to pray, the Holy Spirit filled him and he began speaking in tongues.

Later this small group began to meet in a storefront church in River Rouge, Michigan, which later became the River Rouge Assembly of God. George was the Bible teacher and often preached when the pastor was gone. George and his family became very involved in ministry.

Upbringing and Family

From early childhood, Art grew up in River Rouge Assembly with a girl named Audrey. They fell in love and, when Art was twenty, just out of Bible school, and Audrey was nineteen, they married. Art was asked to preach as a small church in Adrian, Michigan, founded by two women. The church asked him to be their pastor and he accepted, becoming the first full-time pastor of Bethany Assembly of God.

Art and Audrey had four children. In 1953, their oldest, Debbie, was born. Four years later, Rich was born. Then Audrey suffered a miscarriage, but in 1961 their daughter Deana was born. The beautiful little baby was placed in Audrey's arms; however, twenty-four hours later the doctors discovered a serious heart defect. Little Deana was rushed to University of Michigan Hospital and only lived three days.

Audrey was heartbroken at the loss of Deana. Because her pregnancies had all been very difficult, Art and Audrey decided they would have no more children. But, exactly one year later on November 30, Deana's birthday, Doug was born.

Childhood Years

Audrey says that little "Dougie" was delightful—always a joy—a happy child who was never a problem and never had a temper tantrum. He was also energetic. He wanted to start kindergarten a year early at four, but, on advice from the teacher, Art and Audrey didn't let him.

When Doug was five, the church's head usher, Brother Taylor, died. At the funeral dinner in the church fellowship hall, Audrey suddenly noticed that Doug was missing. She looked around and saw Doug at the head of the line with the widow. Audrey thought, *Oh, my goodness!* She started to go after Doug, but the widow saw her and gave her a sign to hold back. The widow later told Audrey that Doug had walked up to her and said, "Sister Taylor, you don't have to be alone anymore, because I will be here to be your man." And he picked up her tray of food and carried it to the table. Audrey says that was when she and Art first realized that Doug had a natural, genuine love for people.

At the age of six, during one Sunday morning church service, Doug went forward when his father gave a salvation invitation. Though his comprehension of what had happened in his life was simple at that young age, one thing was made very clear to him—he needed Jesus as his Savior. His family celebrated his going forward as the greatest decision of his life. He vividly remembers the church altar workers hugging him. He knew by their response how important this was. His parents encouraged him to tell people right away that he had accepted Jesus into his heart.

When Doug was nine, on a Sunday night, his father preached on the baptism in the Holy Spirit. Doug went to the altar to seek the Baptism and received. Shortly after that, his father died. Doug says that he knows it was the fullness of the Spirit that sustained him through the hard times after his father died.

Doug remembers his dad being a strong preacher and a caring, devoted father. He also remembers his dad's fun nature. After Sunday

Left to right: Audrey, Debbie, Rich, Art, and Doug Clay

night service, his dad would go to the A&W drive-in with the two boys, Doug and Rich, in one car, while Audrey drove the other car with Debbie. To the delight of the boys, Art repeatedly played a trick on Audrey at the A&W. He would tell the carhop, "There's a lady over there in a blue Chevrolet. She will try to tell you I will pay her bill. Don't believe her." Then, he and the boys would watch and laugh when the carhop told Audrey that Art wouldn't pay her bill. Audrey says that finally all the carhops at A&W caught on to Art's little game.

Debbie helped both Rich and Doug avoid being disciplined by their parents. If they got in trouble, or if they were arguing and fighting, she would tell them, "Okay, boys. If you kneel down and ask God to forgive you, I won't tell Mom and Dad." So they avoided some spankings because of their sister. And they loved her for it.

Twice Art and Audrey left Doug alone in the church. Each thought that Doug was with the other parent. After arriving home and finding that neither of them had Doug, Art rushed back to the church and found Doug all alone in the church, sleeping on a pew.

Art often took Doug with him to do ministry. Whether it was going to the nursing homes and hospitals, whatever he was doing, he took Doug with him. After Doug grew up and became a minister, Gail says that's what he did with their girls. Even in the busiest times—especially when he was youth director in Ohio, traveling quite a bit, and their kids were small—he always had time to take his daughters with him to do ministry. He would work it into a way that was fun for them. Through those times they developed a love for visiting people in the hospital and going to the nursing homes just as Doug had learned from his dad. Doug would come home and grab one of their daughters and say, "Hey, go with me." It might have been as a simple as going back to his office to get something he needed, but he would make it fun and sound like an exciting adventure. Or he would say something like, "We're gonna do this and maybe get a McDonald's ice cream cone on the way home." What his dad did to include him helped develop in Doug that love for people and ministry that was evident in how he interacted with his own girls.

In 1968, Art prepared to leave Bethany Assembly to be the pastor of Brightmoor Tabernacle in Detroit, Michigan. Brightmoor was the largest AG church in Michigan. The pastor, Bond Bowman, had been elected as superintendent of the Michigan District. Art was voted in by 98 percent of the members. However, before the Clays could move to Detroit, Pastor Bowman came to him and said, "Art, I don't feel it's God's will for me to be the district superintendent. Would you feel bad if I went back to my church?" Art respectfully agreed. Bethany Assembly had not yet found a new pastor, so Art and his family stayed in Adrian. Although disappointing at the time, this event turned out to be good because, when Art passed away, Pastor Bill Leach and Bethany Assembly continued to provide wonderful care for Audrey and her children. Audrey served on staff at Bethany Assembly as minister of music and pastoral care for fifty-five years, retiring at age seventy-five.

The Death of Doug's Dad

About three years after he returned to Bethany, Art wasn't feeling well one night. He had had a heart attack five years before, but he told Audrey, "I can't go to the ER one more time." The next morning, he fell over and Audrey grabbed the nitroglycerin tablets. Art prayed, "Lord, forgive me for not doing more for You in my lifetime!" When he prayed that prayer, Audrey knew it might be the end, but she called an ambulance anyway. At the hospital, a doctor they knew well came out of the ER crying and said, "Audrey, we did everything we could."

Later, Donna Liebler, a close friend of Audrey's from the church, an X-ray technician at the hospital (and the Clays' babysitter) was with Audrey when Art died. She said that Audrey immediately exclaimed, "Oh, my boys, my boys! What'll I do?" Audrey knew it would be hard on Debbie, but she was already at CBC. It would be hardest on the boys, who adored their dad. He was such a devoted father to them and their hero.

Doug's last memory of his dad is from the morning he died. As Doug left for school, he saw his dad huddled in a chair in the living room having his devotions, with an afghan Audrey had knitted for him around his shoulders.

Doug says that his most traumatic experience in life was the death of the father he loved so much. But, it also became his greatest opportunity to see God's hand of faithfulness, which he still draws on today.

At the funeral, one of the officiating ministers was T. E. Gannon. At the viewing, he saw Doug slip something into the pocket of his dad's jacket in the casket. Unbeknownst to Doug, Brother Gannon retrieved that envelope and saved it. On the back of an offering envelope, Doug had written a message. "Dad," he wrote, "don't worry. I will take care of Mom," and signed it. More than ten years later, Doug was in the *Revivaltime* choir with Brother Gannon's granddaughter, Melissa. One day, she handed Doug something. She said, "My mom and dad thought you would want this." Doug recognized the offering envelope with the message he had placed in his dad's jacket in the casket. He still has the note.

Art Clay

Audrey recalls that, when Doug came home from school one day, he looked at Audrey's eyes and knew she'd been crying. He said, "That's okay, Mom. I miss him too. It's all right to cry." She says that he always has had such a sensitivity to her needs.

Just a few months after Art's death, Doug came home from school and immediately got on his bike and rode off. When he returned home later, he came in with packages. Audrey asked him, "Doug, where have you been?"

Doug replied, "I wanted to buy you a present that I thought would help you not miss Dad so much." He had bought Audrey a spool of thread, a loaf of pumpernickel bread, and a little piano-shaped music box.

"Why did you buy these, honey?"

"Well, I know you like to sew, I know you love pumpernickel bread, and I know you love music," Doug replied.

Then Audrey said, "Doug, where did you get the money? I didn't give you any money."

He answered, "Well, I went to the bank." The bank was about three miles from their house.

Audrey said, "But, you don't have an account there."

Doug replied, "I just went up to the lady, and I told her I wanted to draw some money out, and she gave it to me."

Audrey went to the bank the next day and found the teller who had given Doug the money. The teller had recognized Doug's family name because when Art Clay died it had been on the front page of the local newspaper in Adrian. When the teller asked Doug what he wanted the money for, he had replied, "Well, I'm going to buy my mom a present so she'll feel better." The bank teller who gave Doug the money told Audrey, "We couldn't turn him down. We knew he'd lost his father."

Doug says that he never really felt the trauma of being raised by a single mom, because he was a part of a great church. The church people rallied around Doug's family. He tells people he was raised by the church. His mother, Audrey, stayed active as the minister of music on staff at the church, so church life was really a part of his life all through his childhood and teen years. In that church life, God sent a lot of spiritual dads to come and make impressions on Doug. He remembers vividly the Uncle Gene and Aunt Esther Kids Crusade where he felt for the first time the call of God on his life, and that was obviously confirmed through other events, including a junior high camp.

One of the people who most impressed him—the real father figure— was Bill Leach, who became pastor of Bethany Assembly of God after Doug's dad died. Brother Leach would let Doug go with him out to eat whenever there was a guest minister. (Doug could always tell Brother Leach's relationship with the guest minister by where they went to eat. If it was a friend of Brother Leach, they would go back to the Leach home, have pizza, maybe play games and tell stories. If it was a missionary, someone who was passing through, or someone he may not know well, they'd always go to the Pizza Bucket. But if it was a person of real stature, or someone he respected, they would go to Frisch's Big Boy.)

Doug remembers one time as a ten-year-old boy, only about a year or so after his dad passed away, a high-profile evangelist was holding services at Bethany Assembly. And as was the custom, they went out to eat that night after service. The conversation went towards Doug's dad and Bill Leach following Art Clay as pastor. The evangelist made a statement to Bill Leach in Doug's presence, "You know, Brother Leach, Reverend Clay died prematurely—either because there was sin in his life or a lack of faith on his wife's part."

Doug recalls, "I remember being really affected by the evangelist's comments. Bill's car had a bench seat, and he had me right in the middle. After dropping the evangelist off at his hotel, all the whole way home, he had his arm around me reassuring me that my dad was a godly man, that it wasn't sin in his life or a lack of faith on my mom's part. It was God's timing, and our life and times are in His hands. The evangelist's comments could have really damaged my spiritual well-being, but the loving care of a godly shepherd prevented an erroneous, inappropriate comment from affecting me. That's my upbringing. A year and a half after becoming a single-parent home, my pastor helped me process that this was a part of God's plan."

During the years following his dad's death, Doug's Royal Rangers commanders from his church, men of God, filled a critical space and void in his life that he could not have received from any other activity, either in school or in the community. This is why Doug feels so strongly that the priestly responsibility, the role of men in the church, is to be spiritual fathers to those boys whose fathers have left either through death or desertion. Having healthy Royal Rangers leaders be spiritual dads to a culture of fatherless boys will be the answer to the prayers of many moms and grandmothers.

The Teen Years

Doug's mom describes him as definitely outstanding in the youth group, very down-to-earth, and lots of fun. One time, his school's basketball team started practicing on Wednesday nights. His mother told him, "Doug, you can't miss youth group. You just can't. It's vital." They talked, and she said, "What I want you to do, Doug, is to go to your coach. Don't have a cocky attitude. Don't just say, 'Well, I can't.' Just explain it to him." The next Wednesday, he went and said to his coach, "We have our youth group on Wednesday nights, and I feel I should be there. Mom feels I should be there, but I wanted to let you know." That coach looked at him, "Doug, you come to practice, and when it's time for you to leave to be on time for youth group at your church," he said, "I want you out of there." Doug was very respectful to his coach. This man was not a Christian, but he told Doug, "I want you out of there; you just get off the court and go." This gave Doug some insight on how to treat people, and how he should give his testimony. It also helped Doug realize his gift in dealing with people who may not be easy to deal with, to help them feel that he's not coming down on them or not paying attention.

Doug loves sports. Besides basketball, he played football and baseball. Those disciplines helped him, particularly as he began to understand what God's call on his life was, and he became more focused on his desire to go to Bible school, to prepare for pastoral ministry.

One of Doug's fondest memories is playing defensive end and tight end in football during his junior year of high school. The team was playing an away game. It was very cold and very rainy. They came out on the field to begin pregame calisthenics, and there in the visitor stands— those large stands—were only two people. It was Doug's mom, Audrey, and Bill Leach wrapped up in blankets, and holding an umbrella over their heads. They were the only two in the visitor stands, and they sat through that entire nasty, stormy-weather game watching Doug. He recalls, "I remember, I was supposed to be focused on warming up, and I was focused, but some of my friends were saying, 'Hey Clay, look at your mom. What's she doing?' I was so proud that my mom was there. She was my biggest cheerleader, because she was also my biggest disciplinarian and authority figure in my life." Audrey Clay was very supportive of Doug's athletics and never missed a football game during his four years of high school.

During this time, Doug was also active in Teen Talent (now Fine Arts). He was in a singing group—an ensemble of five—two guys and three girls. Of the four years they went to nationals, that small ensemble from Bethany Assembly in Adrian, Michigan, won Teen Talent two years in a row.

The character and lives of Art and Audrey Clay and the mentoring and example of his pastor Bill Leach have significantly influenced Doug's parenting and family life.

According to Doug's wife, Gail, leading his family and leading a healthy church are connected and embedded in who he is as an adult. Considering his extensive traveling—different times zones and various countries—even if he is dead tired, he jumps into whatever the family is doing right at that point when he returns home. She says, "We're in a wonderful season of grandchildren, five under the age of five. Doug comes home from the airport, swings by the kids' home, and picks up a grandkid or two, bringing them to our house to spend the night with us."

Their younger daughter Kaylee says, "My parents have always been there to love me unconditionally—even and especially when I didn't deserve it. They always made sure to help Ashley and me follow the will of God in our lives. And I am now watching that happen in my children's lives with their grandparents."

Doug is a very early riser. His daughter Ashley recalls that, when she was young, sometimes she would wake up early and sneak down the stairs, knowing where she would find her dad. "I knew that if I just saw him for a moment, kneeling with the afghan his mom knitted for him, I would feel safe and could go right back to sleep. Now, as a parent, I fully understand my dad's parenting success. It was his prayer life."

Doug's personal spiritual life is a reflection of his godly parents. Even the final memory of his father has become a part of his life. The life in the Spirit that Doug learned from his parents has been the foundation for his successive steps in ministry that have truly been ordered of the Lord.

God could not have provided Doug a more supportive wife than Gail. A spiritually unhealthy spouse can make for a lot of ministry frustration, but God gave Doug a wonderful helpmate in Gail whom he says "has been a great asset, a complement, and an always-present encouragement in my ministry ventures. The consistency and constancy of Gail's temperament has been a great source of strength to me in ministry. I could not have done what I have accomplished in ministry without her."

With each transition and in each ministry assignment, she has been 100 percent supportive and committed to what God called Doug to do. She has remained constant, faithful, and very supportive with her love and commitment.

Doug explains, "I have deeply respected the spirituality of Gail. That's been demonstrated not only in her timely input with wisdom and discernment, but her ability to join with me in hearing the voice of God as it related to ministry transitions. It has been an absolute joy and delight to be on the journey of life and ministry with Gail. I could not have had a better life partner."

Doug and Gail

Ashley, J.D., Alee, Jaxon, and Callum

Doug and Mason

*Kaylee, Eli, Mason,
and Kinsley*

Audrey and Doug

SECTION 2

ORDERED
STEPS

2

MINISTRY

Bible College and Interning

In 1981, Doug entered Central Bible College in Springfield, Missouri, as a freshman. Although internships were required for only one summer, he wanted to work in a church each summer during his college years. During these internships, he had the opportunity to see pastoral ministry up close and in action.

The summer after his freshman year, he returned to his home church at Bethany Assembly of God in Adrian, Michigan, and did an internship with his pastor, Bill Leach. Doug had the opportunity to sit in on staff meetings and to go with Pastor Leach on hospital and shut-in visits and emergency calls. Watching the pastoral care side of the church leadership, Bill Leach, and other staff ministers helped Doug realize ministry is all about people. "We're called to shepherd people," Doug explains. "I was at a church recently, and I was picked up at the airport by a staff member who didn't know me. After I asked all my introductory questions, I inquired about how things are going. This staff pastor said to me, 'We're in a great season of ministry here. We process fifteen hundred people a week.' And I thought, *Process?! Is this a manufacturing company? We don't process people, we minister to people.* I knew what he was saying, but I hope we don't ever lose the understanding that as pastors we *shepherd* people. I feel that God's calling on my life is to be a shepherd." Doug discovered this observing what his pastors in Adrian had done, and by having the opportunity to go behind the scenes, watching leadership in action for one summer as an intern. "I became convinced that shepherding is what I wanted to give my life to."

During the summers after his sophomore and junior years, Doug went to Athens, Ohio, to work in a church plant, New Life Assembly, with Pastor John Palmer. It was there that he met Gail Deardorff, who was in nursing school.

Gail's family were relatively new to the church. Her mother, Judy, had been in an automobile accident, and Pastor Palmer told Doug, "I'd like you to pay a family visit to the Deardorffs." Doug was on his way to meet some young people to golf, and the Deardorffs lived near the course. So Doug stopped in and introduced himself, "Hi, I'm Doug Clay, and I'm the summer intern. I'm just here to pray with you and let you know we're standing with you and believing God for your full recovery." Little did Doug realize that around the corner sat Gail, studying for some of her nursing classes. As Gail tells the story, she quickly changed her clothes, got spruced up, came around the corner, and said, "Hi, how are you?" And that's where Doug and Gail first met. Doug recruited her to be a youth sponsor and later recruited her for their life's journey together.

Doug and Gail on their wedding day

One incident during his senior year had a significant impact on his leadership perspective and how he approached ministry. Doug was selected to speak for a senior class chapel. He had to submit his message in advance to the Spiritual Life Committee for approval. His message was from the life of Jacob and entitled, "God's Transforming Power." The basic idea was that God gave Jacob a new name, a new walk, and a new power. Doug practiced the message in front of the mirror, writing the word *pause* throughout his sermon notes as a reminder. He had his sermon down to about twenty-two minutes and planned to do an altar call.

After being introduced by President Maurice Lednicky, Doug came to the platform. As he tells it, he was "immediately struck with being nervous. I could feel that my hands were shaking, my body was sweating, and when I started talking, my voice was considerably higher than what it was normally." He started preaching and within eleven minutes, he was done with the whole message. He prayed and gave the altar call. Nobody responded! He led the song, "I Exalt Thee." He even changed keys, and still nobody responded. He sat down, feeling totally dejected—how in the world could he go out and be a preacher, if he couldn't even speak in the college chapel? All of a sudden he felt an arm around his shoulder. He turned and looked; it was Dr. Gary McGee, one of his favorite professors. "You know, Doug, it's so refreshing not to have a marathon sermon in chapel. Way to go, young man!" That word of affirmation planted a seed in Doug to make sure, in his words, "that I'm always affirming of others. I'm always seeking to raise the confidence level of the people that I work and serve with."

Dr. McGee had originally advised Doug that, if he could afford it, he should be involved in ministry each of the summers of his college experience. Hence his internships each summer. Other leadership experiences Doug had on campus were his involvement in Delta Chi and student government. He was also president of the Revivaltime Choir for three years.

Cincinnati Youth Pastor

After Doug graduated in 1985, he served as youth pastor at First Christian Assembly in Cincinnati, Ohio, with Clyde Miller. Doug describes it as a wonderful, first full-time ministry experience. Clyde

Miller became a loving, spiritual father to Doug, allowing him to be youthful and idealistic. To this day, Doug says that his love for people was really influenced by watching Clyde and his wife, Anita, shepherd the people of their flock well, loving them unconditionally. In reflecting on this, Doug said, "If I could say anything to our pastors in the first moments of this administration, it would be to fall in love with the people you're called to lead."

Clyde was also full of energy. Doug recalls a time when he and Clyde were driving to a Teen Challenge banquet. They were running late when they discovered that the road ahead was washed out. They realized there was no way they could cross that washed-out road. But Clyde spotted a picnic table in a yard. Dressed in their suits and ties, they went over and grabbed the picnic table, dropping it down where the water was flowing across the middle of the road. Clyde stepped up on the picnic table, jumped across to the other side, and told Doug, "Put the table back, drive the car around the other way, and meet me at Teen Challenge." When Doug eventually arrived at the banquet, Clyde was standing up front speaking like nothing had ever happened.

Doug was Clyde's youth pastor for two and a half years. He says that, for a young person just out of Bible college, he could not have asked for a better first ministry experience. "I'm well aware of the value of the first experience of some of our ministerial students coming out of college. Pastor Clyde Miller, his wife Anita, and First Christian Assembly gave Gail and me a very positive, healthy, and beneficial first experience in what ministry is about."

Clyde also showed Doug what it meant to be a part of a team. Doug said, "I felt cared for and invested in by the people I worked for. I didn't feel like I was a hireling. That positive experience started with Clyde Miller, and I think that's why I'm so adamant about the team concept." Clyde instilled in Doug that there are certain things that a minister needs to invest in his team to bring out the best in them. Let them operate in the realm of their giftings so no one misses out on their God-given capabilities. Don't "lord it over" any staff person. That makes them feel like a hireling, not a part of the team.

Des Moines Youth Pastor

In 1987, Doug went to First Assembly in Des Moines, Iowa, where he served as youth pastor for two and a half years. This was Doug's first opportunity to be a part of a larger church with multiple staff members. There he discovered the administrative side of pastoring. Until that point, youth ministry had been the big ministry in the church—the youth pastor could do pretty much what he wanted. But in a larger church with multiple staff, there were unique dynamics. It was there that Doug saw the value of administration systems and process. Sometimes young pastors have a tendency not to see the spiritual validity of church process or systems and how they can actually promote growth in the local church. At First Assembly, Doug observed a well-oiled machine that taught him how healthy processes—like the intentionality of focusing on guests and on assimilating people—can make a large church have an intimate feeling among its members, similar to a small church.

One of the most meaningful takeaways that Doug had from his time at First Assembly was watching Pastor John Palmer's strategy of intentionally remembering each person's name, finding those who were in physical or emotional pain, and then meeting people at their point of need. John knew who was going to be in the hospital. Even though it was a large church and sometimes that responsibility was delegated, Pastor Palmer always made sure that the pastoral staff were connecting with people in times of need, trauma, and life interruptions. Through that kind of ministry, Doug became convinced that a person could pastor a large church and still have a personal touch with people.

Ohio District Youth Director

In 1989, Doug was called back to Ohio to serve as the district youth director (DYD). Doug describes that time as a great privilege to work with the district superintendent, Robert Crabtree. Doug had a great love for being on that team and serving the students of Ohio.

The summer of 1989 while Doug was preaching a youth camp at Big Prairie, Ohio, he saw a red Cadillac drive into the camp. Out stepped three men dressed in suits. Doug saw Robert Crabtree, Dr. Richard Dobbins, and Don McManness get out of the car. Doug thought, *Something is going on.* Jim Palmer, the Ohio district youth director, walked up to Doug and said, "Our district brethren are here and they want to see you." Doug's heart sank. He thought, *Oh my word! Am I in trouble? What's happening here?"* He entered the office where the three gentlemen were sitting, and Bob Crabtree, in his stately superintendent voice said, "Brother Clay, the district brethren are here, and we'd like to have a conversation with you." Doug was sure his face must have appeared shocked. Superintendent Crabtree told him that Jim Palmer wanted to plant a church, and they were in the process of searching for the next district youth director.

When the interview was done, Brother Crabtree said, "We feel that this is the will of the Lord. Would you consider being the next DYD?" But Doug was caught off guard. "I'm very honored by this request," he said, "but please, I didn't know this was going to happen. My family is not even aware of this. I serve on staff at a church. Would you give me the opportunity to go back and talk to my pastor?"

When Doug returned to Des Moines, he went to talk to his pastor. Pastor Palmer said, "I certainly would hate to see you leave, but if you feel this is the will of the Lord, then we want the will of the Lord for you." Doug kept praying, but couldn't sense God's direction. Doug describes it this way: "It was as though a traffic light wouldn't turn red or green—it just stayed yellow." He went back in to talk to Pastor Palmer about how he was feeling, and John told him, "I can't be the voice of the Lord for you, but it's obvious that the spiritual authority in Ohio feels that you're their person. If you want to listen to that spiritual authority, I believe that God will honor your choice to follow their advice." Based on that counsel, Doug accepted the Ohio District's invitation. Shortly after that, Doug's sister, Debbie, told him that in a family camp in Minnesota, during one particular moment in a service, she had felt an impression that she needed to slip away and pray for her brother. And when they checked, it was at the exact time Doug was being interviewed by the Ohio leadership at their campground.

Through this experience, Doug learned even more about the importance of spiritual authority's counsel for his life.

In describing Doug's time as DYD, Robert Crabtree said:

> One of Doug's strengths was that he had the ability to build on what his predecessor had done. He was energetic, excited, and had a tremendous cooperative spirit. Jim Palmer had done a great job; the youth conventions had been about fifteen hundred or so and Jim got them up around twenty-five hundred. Then Doug built the youth convention up to over five thousand. All of the district youth programs really accelerated. Doug had the ability to build rapport at every level. He made the small church feel important—they felt included—it wasn't just the big churches. He liked to spend time together. He would come to me and say, "Hey, can I drive you to the business meeting?" And we would just spend some time one-on-one. He always seized every opportunity to learn.

Doug related:

> Some of my fondest ministry experiences that I cherish to this day were when I was serving as a district youth director—not just because I worked with great leadership like Brother Crabtree and Dr. Dobbins, but when you think about the significance that youth directors play in this Fellowship, I carry a strong burden for the next generation. I believe there is no better environment for Assemblies of God young people to experience the baptism in the Holy Spirit and the challenge of the call of God on their life than in youth camps. I believe, spiritually speaking, through youth camps, district youth directors have the highest return on investment for long-term ministry fruitfulness. I saw that, and I had leadership that really celebrated that. For seven and a half years, it was our privilege to oversee youth ministries in the state

of Ohio, sponsoring youth camps and missions trips. To this day I run across people in the Fellowship who say, "Hey, you were my district youth director in Ohio."

As general superintendent, I want our district youth directors and youth pastors to feel valued, affirmed—for them to feel from me that I view the student culture not just as the church of tomorrow, but very much as the church of today.

I don't want my leadership to be based on personal preference styles that create a ministry the next generation has to undo to be effective. So, I want to help build the future of this church with young people in mind. After all, David said, "Lord, don't forsake me when I'm old and grey until I declare your power to the next generation." You and I have had our Pentecost, but there's a generation of young people that desperately need their Pentecost. I want to see it happen in Assemblies of God churches and camps.

One of the highlights that Doug had as DYD was being able to speak to cultural issues with real biblical answers. In one youth convention, Doug challenged the young people and the youth leaders from the Scripture to lay aside every weight of sin that would keep them from fulfilling their God-given purpose. He arranged to have burn barrels placed in the auditorium prior to service. He told the students, "If you have anything in your possession right now that would keep you from serving God, I want you to come and throw those things in this barrel. We're going take them out and burn them." The kids came and threw in cigarettes, marijuana, condoms, and pornographic pictures they had in their wallets. Some teens put in notes about sinful activities that they had planned to do during the convention. One girl threw in two razor blades. She had been cutting as a way of coping. It was a powerful, spiritual moment as they filled two barrels.

In another youth convention in Cincinnati, Ohio, Doug felt impressed of the Lord to teach on the subject of moral purity, particularly in the area of abstinence and saving oneself for marriage. Registration was record-breaking—with over forty-five hundred youth in attendance. He had done a tour with Josh McDowell, the *Why Wait?* Tour. And, Doug had been preaching a message entitled, "Teens Need Convictions, Not Contraceptives"—the whole concept was that Gideon Bibles had been replaced by Planned Parenthood's condom distribution. Doug wanted to bring back a biblical understanding of moral purity.

In this particular youth service, Doug challenged the junior high and high school students to live a life of moral purity. He had obtained some little gold bar pins worn on varsity jackets or sweaters to indicate the years of lettering in a sport. The point of his message was that "moral purity is like a gold bar. It's one of those commodities that appreciates in value. If you will use it for its intended purpose, it will bring great blessing into your life." After the message, Doug's wife read a charge and prayed for the girls; then he read a charge and prayed for the boys. Doug and Gail challenged the students: "Keep this gold bar, and someday when you stand at an altar, in addition to exchanging rings, build into the ceremony that you're giving your moral purity to your future mate." Those gold bars had a great impact on the students.

Several years later, while pastoring in Toledo, Ohio, Doug was conducting premarriage counseling for a couple. At the end, as Doug and the young bride-to-be were creating the order of service, she told him, "Pastor Clay, you may not remember this, but I was a student at the youth convention when you challenged us to save ourselves for a future day and a future spouse." Then she pulled out the gold bar, "I'd like to give you my gold bar and ask you to make it a part of our wedding ceremony." Unbeknownst to the groom-to-be, when Doug got to the ring exchange part of the wedding, he gave the young man the gold bar and challenged him: "Today, not only are you getting a ring that signifies her unending love, you're getting a gold bar that represents a commitment she made to keep herself pure for you and this day." What an impact a little gold bar and a challenge to remain pure had on that young woman!

As DYD, Doug also took groups of teens on missions trips. One trip took them to Neuquén, Argentina. He divided the group into three teams with each team going to different places of ministry. He assigned one youth pastor to preach. (That was part of Doug's ministry style as DYD, giving youth pastors the opportunity to lead and preach at district events.) While the team was praying after the sermon at one church, one student felt impressed to pray for a particular man in a wheelchair, that God was going to heal him. The student went to Doug, and Doug told him, "Well, if you feel this is God, go for it." These high school students gathered around the man and began praying with such intensity. After some time, Doug thought, *Okay, it's about time for me to go over and explain God's sovereignty and that He doesn't always heal how and when we want Him to.* And he began to walk over to the group. At that moment, Doug saw this high school student step back, shake his head with a quizzical look that said, "How come this isn't happening?" Then he stepped back, put his hands again on the man, and started praying, "In the name of Jesus, I pray that you would rise up and walk." When he used the phrase, "Rise up and walk," the man jumped out of his wheelchair and began running and leaping the length of the entire church. God showed himself powerful to the students, that church, and the youth pastor. God was faithful to a young man's prayer and let them be a part of a miracle.

National Youth Director

In 1995, Thomas Trask, the general superintendent, invited Doug to come to the national offices in Springfield as the national youth director.

That year was a General Council year, and while Doug was still the DYD of the Ohio District, he was asked to fill in temporarily for the vacant national position. Brother Trask had a passion to do more in the city of Saint Louis, Missouri, than just have a General Council. He really wanted to have an evangelistic outreach. It was called, "The Gateway of Hope," a large outreach, mobilizing several thousand youth who were there for the Fine Arts Festival. They hit the streets to do evangelism and to work in churches. Since then, there has been some sort of outreach associated with each General Council. It started with a dream in Brother Trask's heart, and Doug felt it a great privilege to be a part of seeing that dream fulfilled.

After the 1995 General Council, Brother Trask called Doug: "I really feel this in my heart. What would it take to have you on the team?" Doug replied, "You know, Brother Trask, I think I can do more for you here in Ohio than I can there." Doug explained that his perception was that there might be some institutional barriers at the national office that, over time, had run their useful course. But Brother Trask committed himself to open the door for Doug to make change if he would be the person to lead that change. And Doug immediately felt in his spirit that he should accept Brother Trask's invitation.

One of the assignments of being the national youth director was to create change that was more field relevant. And in a short amount of time, the Lord gave Doug favor with district youth directors and with pastors. At the Indianapolis General Council in 1997, Doug preached the Friday night service on the call of God. He arranged to have golden cords that would represent the call of God. During the service, these golden cords were placed on those young people who felt a call of God on their lives. Interestingly, this year at General Council when Doug was elected general superintendent, a young pastor came up to him and said, "You don't know me, but I was in that service in Indianapolis when you talked about the call of God. That's where I experienced my call into ministry at the 1997 General Council, and I'm here today, twenty years later, in 2017, voting for you as my general superintendent."

According to Doug, the influence of Brother Trask's leadership is still very evident in his life today. Brother Trask had such a strong imprint of being a leader with strength and courage, yet a spiritual dimension and a deep spiritual discernment. In addition, he operated prophetically. Doug said, "I learned that you could be a strong decisive leader, yet have a very spiritual dimension to your leadership. It was a great, great experience. You could tell when Brother Trask was resolved, that he'd heard from God. And that's one of my takeaways from sitting under his leadership. I don't want to overpromise and underdeliver, I hope to open the door for people here to have ministry dreams flourish."

Toledo Pastorate

In 1997, at the Indianapolis General Council service, Doug was approached by Robert Crabtree and Don McManness of the Ohio District who asked if Doug would consider coming to Calvary Assembly of God in Toledo, Ohio, to pastor. Calvary was a wounded church at the time. The church had gone through a lot of tragedies, particularly in the way in which pastors left. It was four million dollars in debt. It was district supervised and the board had been displaced. It was a hurting, hurting church. But in spite of all of its problems, Doug felt that God had called him and Gail to pastor this hurting church.

"I've seen the gifts of wisdom, knowledge, and a spiritual impartation of discernment in Doug Clay's life probably more than anyone else that I've known or been privileged to interact with in ministry. He clearly has the spiritual gift of leadership."
—Chad Gilligan, pastor, Calvary Assembly of God, Toledo, Ohio

Doug held seven business meetings that first year just to deal with some of the issues. His last one that first year was to try to put the board back into place. When a church is district supervised, the board is dismantled, and the district becomes the board of that church. A lot of the previous board members were hurting badly. One had contacted a lawyer and felt that the district did not have the legal means for its actions. The board member was planning to bring litigation against the Ohio District. That shows how wounded this church was. Doug felt very strongly that God had spoken to him about putting the board back into place so the church could become a sovereign church again.

Although some of Doug's spiritual mentors had told him not to allow certain persons to be on that board, he could not escape the fact God had spoken to him: "Trust the process, trust Me, and let people prove themselves to you as their new pastor." So in that seventh business meeting, there were eighteen nominees to fill a ten-member board. Doug had decided the church needed to trust the Lord and he allowed previous board members' names to be on the ballot. It was thought that it would take five or six ballots to get the required number of votes for the ten board members, being confident that six would be voted in right away. So before the annual church business meeting, the church spent time in prayer. And it was just like God that on the very first ballot of eighteen names, exactly ten received the necessary number of votes—not eleven, not nine, but ten—to be elected. There were enough blank ballots to have six votes, but only one ballot was needed. Doug learned a valuable lesson through this: "I learned at Toledo Calvary that it's God's church! It's not a business with a steeple on top to be tweaked by a bunch of engineers. It is *His* church. Trust Him. "

According to Chad Gilligan, his former children's pastor (currently pastoring Toledo Calvary), Doug also has a gift of affirming and giving value to others.

I've watched him do it, whether it was a senior saint in the church who needed to know that their pastor cared for them or a child he interacted with to create a memory. If a person was questioning their faith or someone who was a longtime church member was having problems, he would know how to help that person. On one occasion, a member of the church had done something incredibly irresponsible. Four staff members were talking about it, trying to decide what to do. As we were trying to figure out what to do and how we should treat this person, Pastor Clay said, "You guys, they have a soul, and God's called us to care for that person, so we need to keep that in mind as we decide how to respond."

That was very significant to me as a young pastor. I've gone back to that many times. When I'm frustrated with somebody in the church, because their behavior doesn't match my expectation,

I have an immediate tendency to want to dismiss that person, almost to get myself off the hook from my pastoral obligation. But then I hear Doug Clay's voice in my head saying, "You know, guys, they have a soul, and it's our role as pastor before God to care for that person."

When Doug is asked about his journey in leading a hurting church back to health, he says, "The two most common phrases that got me further ahead while I was in those early days of pastoring were this: 'I don't know' and 'Can you help?' When they asked me a question, I didn't try to fake it. I said, 'I don't know' or 'Can you help?' And it was amazing how people came rallying around me when I was honest."

Doug believes that pastoring Toledo Calvary was at the heart of his ministry calling, as well as a vital step to prepare him for the future.

That's where I feel my calling is. I really feel a pastoral calling on my life—leading Calvary, accepting a hurting church, leading it to a point of thriving, and today it's one of our megachurches in the Fellowship. There's no doubt that those experiences in that local church not only shaped my leadership, but also prepared me for district and national leadership. It was at Toledo Calvary that I quickly discovered what I believe God's will was specifically for Toledo Calvary—not to compare itself with any other church. That was freeing for me, and I believe I can take that understanding into the role of general superintendent for our churches across the Fellowship.

When dealing with churches in some agricultural or other small communities, we need to define for them what it means to be a church of influence. I highly value megachurches and the great impact they make on their communities. But the majority of our churches that make up the Assemblies of God are not megachurches, they're smaller churches—and every Assemblies of God church can be a church of influence.

I'm the product of a lot of peoples' investment. In my first year in Toledo when I preached messages on missions, I tried to sound like Dan Betzer. When I was doing expository preaching, I tried to sound like John Lindell. I was a product of all of these people whom I admire. But it's interesting, the momentum became noticeable and sustainable when I got comfortable in my skin— not just for who I was, but for who I wasn't. When I discovered who I wasn't, I didn't have to copy and paste the model of other churches and leaders; I could lead according to the gifts God gave me for Toledo Calvary.

Ohio District Superintendent

In 2004, Doug became the Ohio District superintendent. He was in his early forties. He had worked earlier in his ministry as the Ohio district youth director, under a real spiritual icon, Robert Crabtree.

Doug felt a real conviction that the district office needed to transition from being a sort of command and control center to a relationship resource and releasing of ministry center. It seemed as if districts had served their useful time in being event-driven and event-sponsoring centers. Due to the health, growth, and maturity of many local churches inside districts and networks, the ways they serve and resource these churches have changed. Many districts are incorporating changes to effectively do this. The Ohio District created a byline that says, "Every church's purpose is our priority." Once when Doug was asked, "What's your vision for the district?" he said, "I have about 280 of them, because I feel like our purpose is to help each individual church carry out its mission and its vision." This ideology is how the district leaders came up with the mission statement for the Ohio District— To Resource Ministers and Churches for Health and Growth—and began the transformation into the Ohio Ministry Network.

In having to deal with some of the church problems while district superintendent, Doug said there are two things that had made a great impression on him:

First, I am deeply grateful for the upbringing in a healthy church, and really, it's not about how large the church is; it's about how healthy and how influential it is. The second takeaway I had, as it relates to the church, is I personally don't believe that every church is called to be a megachurch, and every pastor is not equipped to be a megachurch pastor. But every church can be a church of influence, so make sure you're measuring your effectiveness with an appropriate scorecard. A large megachurch scorecard is not going to be the same as for a church that's in an agricultural community. That's what I felt the district could do. We could come alongside and recognize the context in which our churches were and help resource them for health and growth.

John Wootton, who served with Doug as the Ohio District executive secretary and then succeeded him as district superintendent, says, "God's Word is so heavily entrenched in Doug's DNA. That's what I love. The Word of God guides his decisions. The Word of God comes out, not only in what he preaches and how he writes, but just in daily conversations. Doug has an unflinching default to let God's Word and the wisdom of the Holy Spirit just be his natural reaction in every situation."

General Treasurer

James Bridges resigned as general treasurer in January 2008, effective at the end of the fiscal year, March 31. It was the responsibility of Dr. George O. Wood, the general superintendent, to fill the vacancy. According to Dr. Wood, he wasn't looking for a specific skill set, but a spiritual leader who would have the ability to minister in the churches and districts of the Assemblies of God and become a person of influence. The only person he thought of was Doug Clay.

Doug was offered to have his name submitted for two open positions in 2007—general secretary and executive director of U.S. Missions. He felt in his spirit that those ministry assignments were not right for him at that time. Doug had just been elected the executive presbyter for the Great Lakes Region.

When Dr. Wood called him and asked him to prayerfully consider the position, Doug said that he believed he could better serve Dr. Wood as a district superintendent. He even sent Dr. Wood an e-mail with ten reasons why he probably shouldn't be general treasurer. Yet Dr. Wood kept approaching him.

Although Doug had the financial acumen for the position of general treasurer, that's not the primary reason Dr. Wood believed Doug was right for the responsibility. Dr. Wood had something specific in mind when he asked Doug to let his name stand as a possible candidate to fill the role: "Is this the kind of person I would want other people to be like? If a person doesn't have an imitable life, it doesn't matter what skills they have." Dr. Wood considered Doug to be that kind of person—someone others could emulate.

During this time, no one on Doug's team in the Ohio District office knew he was having these conversations with Dr. Wood. Doug had pretty much decided that responsibility wasn't for him. In January 2008, Doug was with his team on their annual retreat to pray and seek God about the next four years when their agenda was derailed. This is how Doug tells it:

> It was John Wootton, Rod Iberg, our CFO at the time, and me. We got away to pray and seek God. John gave a devotion. He opened the Bible and started reading some Scripture. Then we prayed and started with our first question, "What do we see as the preferred future for the Ohio District?" Our CFO kind of flippantly said, "Well, the future might be a little cloudy if Doug Clay gets tapped to be the general treasurer to replace James Bridges." I kind of put that off, when John looked at me and said, "Has that happened?" I just froze. John had not known. Rod had just thrown out a little comment. I said, "All right, guys. Here it is. Yeah, I was contacted by Dr. Wood, but Gail and I haven't even downloaded and processed it yet." John Wootton closed his Bible and said, "We can't go any further until you get a

sense of resolve about this and where you're going." So that time of looking four years ahead turned into a time of prayer for me to be able to discern the will of the Lord.

Dr. Wood wanted to submit Doug's name as the nominee to the Executive Presbytery in their January 2008 meeting. Doug had some concerns and was uncertain. Brother Wood suggested that he fly to Springfield on the day before the Executive Presbytery meeting so the two of them could sit together and talk about it.

Dr. Wood said, "I feel strongly in my spirit that I want you on this team. I'm not asking you just to be the national bean counter; I'm interested in your leadership acumen that would build bridges to districts, build bridges to some of the younger leaders. I'm asking you to prayerfully consider letting me submit your name." After Doug prayed overnight, he decided to let his name stand. He assumed the completion of Brother Bridges' two-year unexpired term, but stayed as the Ohio District superintendent for four more months so there would be a successful transition to the new superintendent in Ohio, John Wootton.

Doug brought excellent leadership skills to the office of general treasurer. And he's been a loyal supporter of the office of the general superintendent, walking through some difficult times with Dr. Wood. In terms of things Doug had to do in the Executive Leadership Team as general treasurer, he has always been supportive and candid in offering his advice. Dr. Wood explains:

> Sometimes, I've had to pull it out of him, because he didn't want to interject himself into how he would do something versus how I would do it. He has been extraordinarily respectful to me as a leader. I value him as a friend and the influence he has in our Movement. It's very clear that he is loved throughout the Fellowship. I will do everything I can to help make his administration successful.

Of Dr. Wood's leadership, Doug said:

> The commitment that Dr. Wood has to the centrality of Christ and the Word of God is so very strong. There's no doubt that during his administration, Dr. Wood had to make some tough decisions. However, the accomplishments in terms of diversity represented in leadership, and the growth of women in the ministry will be appreciated for years to come. He's had the ability to see some of those early passions, some of those things that he felt strongly about, come into fruition under his leadership. I also appreciate that Dr. Wood would not be quick to judge, but he would allow other people to speak into the process. I've probably never met a more intelligent person who makes it easy for people who don't have his intelligence to be around and to speak into his life and the process.

When looking at the leadership of both Dr. Wood and Doug Clay, what many people may not know is the great sense of humor they both have, and they rib one another a lot. One time, Doug told Dr. Wood that the reason why the finances were in the red in a particular cost center was that the hospitality expenses for Alton Garrison, the assistant general superintendent, were way out of control. And Dr. Wood said, "Are you serious? Are you serious? I know he likes to eat at nice restaurants." Doug said, "Hey, Chief, I'm just teasing." Not too long after, in an Executive Leadership Team meeting where Doug wasn't present, the ELT produced a fake set of minutes. In them, they approved funding for several erroneous projects. When Doug read those "minutes," he almost had a heart attack and shot an e-mail to everyone, "How come I wasn't in the loop on such and such?" And Dr. Wood's reply to Doug was, "Gotcha!"

There's also a college football rivalry between Dr. Wood and Doug. Dr. Wood is a University of Southern California (USC) fan and Doug is an Ohio State fan. One year these two teams were both highly ranked. While Dr. Wood was on a cruise with his family and Doug was at a men's conference with 450 men, Doug posted Dr. Wood's cell phone number on the video screen and said, "Guys, would you do me a favor? For this number that's on the screen, could you text right now a message like, 'Go Buckeyes!' or 'The general treasurer is doing a great job!'" Dr. Wood's phone just started lighting up and buzzing, and he had over three hundred text messages from people he didn't know. Doug had told the guys, "Now watch this, we'll get a call in just a few minutes." And sure enough, Dr. Wood surmised it was Doug and called him. Sometimes we may get the impression that our leaders are all business, but this shows the approachability and authenticity of those God has chosen to lead this Fellowship.

During his time as general treasurer, Doug discovered that he could stay connected to the local church even at that level of leadership. He explains,

> It's not about being so far removed that you can't relate. It's all about the attitude of the heart. I stay connected to the local church. I stay involved with my mentoring group on the field. When I attend church on Sundays and I'm not in ministry, I'm looking, I'm studying. You do not have to fall out of love with the church when you get into these broader administrative roles in our ecclesiastical structure.

> I'm grateful to say that I have worked with fellow executive officers who have a great love for the local church. I enjoyed it when, sitting around the table, we would ask questions like, "How does this play out in the local church?" And I don't see that changing. I really do think that if what we do does not strengthen the effectiveness of the local church, we've really got to evaluate it. The Assemblies of God is a church movement that's heavily influenced by the office of the pastor.

> I also think there's an apostolic calling when we are on the field in weekend ministries. I'm not looking to just be the guest minister that has to be honored—we come in and receive all this culture

Left to right: Thomas E. Trask, Doug Clay, and George O. Wood

of honor. I believe we are to come in and be a complementary voice to what God is saying in that local situation. When our team goes out, it's not so much about being hosted, but it's about asking the question, "How well are we serving you?" I just came from a leadership meeting, and I told our leadership team, "I'm letting people in our churches say, 'Congratulations! Let us know how we can serve you' until October 8. But after October 8, our cadence is going to be, 'How can *we* serve *you?*'"

"Doug is a person of sterling character—a person of conviction. I know from working with him closely that he is not one to make a hasty decision, but gives thorough thought to his decision making and will seek whatever counsel he needs in the process."
—Thomas Trask, General Superintendent of
the Assemblies of God, 1993–2007

As a pastor, youth pastor, and general treasurer, Doug has formed friendships beyond the church world. For eight years, he has golfed regularly with a group of non-AG guys. When in town, that group has been his social network. His friend Dan Burns says, "Bringing Doug into the golf group was a very natural thing, because all those guys, whether Christian or not, love golf and other sports. Doug was able to join the group and show them what a Christian leader truly looks like. Because of Doug's influence, guys have come to know Christ and several now regularly attend church."

Doug says, "Friendships with people outside the church are critical. I enjoy having 'God talks' with my pre-Christian friends, and walking with them through some challenging life issues." Doug

and both of his predecessors believe that, as the leader of the Fellowship, the primary role of a general superintendent is pastoral. Brother Trask believes the superintendent has to be available to the pastors to serve their spiritual well-being, because the church will only rise to the level of the pastor's spirituality.

Dr. Wood expresses it this way, "It falls to the general superintendent to model the true work of an under-shepherd to feed, guide, protect, and love so that when 'the Chief Shepherd appears, you will receive the crown of glory that will never fade away'" (1 Peter 5:4).

Lessons Learned in Ministry

When asked what are the most important lessons he learned in ministry, Doug responded:

In any leadership position I've held, I've tried to make sure I had spirituality, integrity, and humility.

Spirituality—I just want to stay in love with Jesus. In this position, I must continue to grow in my relationship with Jesus!

When I talk about **integrity**, I'm not just talking about morals. I get that. I want to have an integrity of motives. I want my motives to be pure. I'm rereading Dr. Gary McGee's book, *People of the Spirit*, and I've particularly been fixed on the previous twelve general superintendents. This morning I wept as I read about some of the personal sacrifices that E. N. Bell made. Almost all of my predecessors have had to sacrifice something coming into this position, and that is overwhelming to me. It is overwhelming to know that I am now in a seat that was made possible because of the tremendous sacrifice of some of our past leaders.

In reading the history of the Assemblies of God, I'm amazed at not only the sacrifice, but at the ability to act in faith with initiatives that were much bigger than the people involved. For example, consider the launch of *Revivaltime*. To be a syndicated radio broadcast of ABC, that's phenomenal. That would be like us having a television show on Fox or some other network today. There wasn't just a sacrifice by these early leaders, but they operated out of faith, according to the vision God had put in their hearts. That, quite frankly, is daunting and challenging to me.

Third, **humility**. And I was sincere when I said at General Council that I want the applause for George Wood to be greater than for my acceptance. I've learned, not only from Dr. Wood, but I've learned all my life, that our predecessors in the Assemblies of God have laid a foundation strong enough to bear the weight of future growth and future development. And I don't want to mess that up. Our leaders in the past not only laid foundations, but they also built some great structures—they were people of great vision and faith.

I am convinced that our legacy will be what we model. As you look at the leadership of the past twelve general superintendents, it's quite obvious that each one has a legacy. These leaders each added to the foundation that is bearing the weight of the growth for the Assemblies of God today—an enduring result of their legacy.

I pray that the legacy of my leadership would be known as spirituality, integrity, and humility.

SECTION 3

ORDERED
STEPS

3

PRIORITIES AND PASSIONS

INTRODUCTION

Doug's Priorities and Passions

Shortly after his election as general superintendent, Doug Clay was asked what his vision is for the Assemblies of God. Doug replied, "I can't know that yet, really. Vision comes with authority, and that mantle has not yet been placed on me."

However, when I asked Doug what his priorities and passions are, in less than a minute—speaking from his heart—he listed the six things you will read about in this section. Subsequently, I interviewed him about each of them. The following are his extemporaneous responses in his own words.

While he seeks and expects the Spirit to guide him with the vision God has for the Assemblies of God, these priorities and passions will undoubtedly be reflected in the actions and initiatives that will emerge in our Fellowship under Doug's leadership.

—Randy Hurst

BIBLICAL LITERACY

The word *worldview* gets thrown around a lot. An individual's worldview is a comprehensive perspective from which they see and interpret life. It's kind of an elusive word. How you perceive something is influenced by where you come from and your experiences.

Everybody has a worldview, but I contend a biblical worldview is far more important. Perceiving and interpreting the realities of life through the lens of Scripture will keep you from being misled. Your worldview is shaped by your family and friends, your life experiences, the media, and social media or networks. The fact is, none of these sources offers a completely fair and balanced perspective. A biblical worldview, however, leads us to moral absolutes and to the realities of miracles, redemption, and human dignity. You say, "Doug, do you really believe that strongly in the Word of God being foundational for everything?" Yes, I do, because I believe God has both the integrity and the ability to deliver on His Word and His promises.

Think about it: When someone is the victim of a broken promise, it's either because the one making the promise did not have the integrity to follow through on their promise, or they lacked the ability or resources to back up the promise. But thankfully, God has both integrity and ability. He will follow through on everything He says in His Word, and His ability and His resources guarantee complete fulfillment of His promises.

I discovered firsthand God's integrity and ability relating to His promises during my freshman year in Bible college. I am a third-generation Pentecostal preacher's kid; yes, I was born and raised in the Assemblies of God. I grew up in the church; I cut my teeth on the back of church pews!

When I was nine years old, my dad died suddenly of a heart attack—my brother was fifteen, and my sister was eighteen. My dad was only forty-one years old when he passed away. I never felt the negative impact of being raised by a single mom. You see, long before the phrase "spiritual father" became popular, I had a host of spiritual dads. I had Royal Rangers commanders who helped me build my Derby car; I had "dads" in youth group who took me on campouts or to Detroit Tigers baseball games. I felt sorry for the kids who only had one dad.

When I felt the call of God on my life, I chose to come to Central Bible College to chase this ministry dream. At CBC I met other kids whose dads were pastors. Up and down the dorm hall, I was meeting preacher's kids.

One of my hallmates was a preacher's kid from Illinois. On weekends, he would go home and participate in the service or be part of church life for that weekend. When he came back to school, we'd stay up late on Sunday night talking church stuff. He'd say things like, "My dad said this is how we ought to do evangelism," "My dad says this is how we ought to assimilate people," or "My dad says this is how we ought to equip people for ministry." Those statements had an impact on me and began to shift my thinking.

For the first time in my life, I felt I had been cheated by God. I thought, *Lord, I would like a dad who would walk out these spiritual things with me; I would like a dad who would mentor me in pastoral philosophy.* I started to develop a negative attitude toward God. I thought, *Lord, you've cheated me here. You took my dad from me. Why would You do something so unjust to our family? Why would You leave me fatherless?*

This mind-set of an unjust God lingered with me, so much so that I was ready to quit school, go home, and just take care of my mom. I couldn't figure out why God would do something like this. I remember calling my mom one evening and saying, "Mom, I can't put this together. Can you connect the dots for me? Why would God do something so unjust and unfair to our family?"

As only a godly, wise pastor's wife and mom could do, my mom said to me, "Honey, I can't answer your whys, but I can promise you this," and she broke into a beautiful prayer. Her prayer went something like this: "Lord, You said in Your Word . . ." That prayer stands out forever in my memory, but let me tell you, my mom had used that phrase "*Lord, you said . . .*" a lot while I was growing up.

In this critically important prayer, she was spot-on, because she said, "Lord, You said in Your Word that You'd be a Father to the fatherless, and I claim that reality for my son Doug."

We hung up, and I didn't feel any better. A couple days later, in a Friday night missions service, when the missionary gave the call to come forward, the students were singing, "I'll go where You want me to go, dear Lord," but I didn't move. I just turned around and knelt at my chapel seat. By this time, I wasn't even praying; I was just venting frustration to God. I was saying things like, "God, this stinks. God, this is not fair. Why would You do something like this to me and my family?"

Suddenly I felt the strength and warmth of this huge hand placed on my back. I turned and saw Coach Forrest Arnold—a 6-foot, 6-inch, 250-pound hulk of a man. He had his hand on my back. When I looked him in the face, I saw this big tear coming down his cheek. He said to me, "Doug, I knew your dad, and I know your mom, and both would be really proud of you. And I just want you to know that as long as you're at Central Bible College, I consider you like my own son." Well, when he said "son," I jumped up, and he hugged me, and like instant replay going off in my mind, my mom's prayer came back to me: "Lord, You said in Your Word that You'd be a Father to the fatherless."

From that day forward, I have never doubted God's integrity or His ability to deliver on His Word.

God is infallible; and so is His Word. That's why we embrace 2 Timothy 3:16 so strongly: "All Scripture is God-breathed and useful for teaching, rebuking, correcting and training in righteousness." I embrace the Bible so strongly, because when life doesn't make sense, God's Word gives us stability. Paul said in Philippians 4:6 (GNT), "Don't worry about anything, but in all your prayers ask God for what you need, always asking Him with a thankful heart." I embrace God's Word so strongly, because we live in a time when society places a higher value on tolerance than it does truth. However, God's Word *is* truth. John wrote in 1 John 4:1, "Dear friends, don't believe everything you hear. Carefully weigh and examine everything people tell you. Not everyone who talks about God comes from God."

Learning the Bible, knowing the Bible, and having a worldview shaped by the Bible is so important. And in my life, even in spiritual leadership, there is nothing more effective to anchor my emotions and protect my thinking when I'm going through difficult challenges than God's Word.

PERPETUATING PENTECOST

I recently reread *People of the Spirit: The Assemblies of God,* Gary McGee's classic study of the lives of people who, out of their own Pentecostal experience, shaped who we are today. The Assemblies of God's narrative is one of ordinary people of all ages who have done extraordinary things through the power of the Holy Spirit. Skeptics may dismiss the Pentecostal message and experience, but in every century of the Church Age, Pentecostals have trusted the promises of Scripture and testified about what God has done in their lives.

When many Protestants declared that miracles had ceased with the first-century church, it was Pentecostals who fasted and prayed for the sick and the demon-possessed, and then watched as God proved His willingness to step into human lives to bring healing and deliverance. David prayed in Psalm 71:18, "Even when I am old and gray, do not forsake me, my God, till I declare your power to the next generation, your mighty acts to all who are to come." In the same way, I want to see the many in my generation who have experienced their Pentecost share that experience with succeeding generations. I have a focused passion for seeing Millennials and other younger generations have *their* Pentecost.

This is a challenge for the Assemblies of God today because many churches have lost some of the key opportunities needed in order to perpetuate Pentecost. Having multiple services close together to serve large congregations makes it challenging to offer the needed time for an altar response to a message. Sunday night services often go in a different direction. Sunday School and other legacy programs have either been radically changed or eliminated.

Here's my concern: that the lack of Pentecostal experiences will have an impact on our Pentecostal effectiveness and outcome. We must find and create space for Pentecostal experiences to happen. Two of these critically important interactions with the Spirit I feel deeply concerned for are the baptism in the Holy Spirit and the Spirit's discernable call into Christian service.

When I was growing up, I regularly sought out times at our church's altar. And, while seeking God myself, an elder in our church, a man or woman of God, would always come around and pray for me.

Such a prayer might have sounded like this: "Oh God, I know the plans that You have for Dougie Clay, and I pray that You'll make clear what Your will is for his life."

Those prayers were gold in my life. I grew up with this reinforced sense that God had a calling, even a specific ministry calling, on my life. Our young people need that today. I carry a deep concern that we may be allowing our children and young people to grow up within our churches without challenging them to give their lives in full-time Christian service, either in the ministry or in a missions assignment.

I get it. The ground is level at the Cross, and all of us who have been saved are called to Christian service. But that common identification with all the members of the body of Christ does not rule out the specific purposes and plans the Holy Spirit has in mind for each member of the Body. I am specifically looking for and believing for a great harvest of students and young people who, at an early age, sense the call of God to go into Christian service. But those of us who are already farther along in our journey of service to the Lord must be intentional in guiding and inviting young men and women to embark on their own journeys.

I would appeal to pastors, youth leaders, and Sunday School teachers — anyone with spiritual "reach" into a young person's life — to creatively find space and opportunity for this to happen. If we limit students' potential for this kind of challenge to just a summer camp or summer retreat experience, we are missing out on so many avenues in which we could see their lives transformed. Something as simple as participatory prayer or a group prayer setting can begin to open a young person's attention to new spiritual vistas. You might take it to the next level with an all-church prayer meeting or a twenty-four-hour prayer and fasting emphasis. We must engage our young people in participatory prayer, in spiritually nurturing events, in revival meetings—whatever the mechanism, our kids need time in the presence of the Lord and need our participation to help them discern God's will for their lives.

I was blessed to grow up in an immersive Christian environment where I sensed God's call on my life early on. But that calling crystallized during a junior high camp at Fa-Ho-Lo Park camp in Michigan. The evangelist's name was Michael Brown, and he talked about God's call and that sense of direction. I remember going to the altar and feeling so strongly that God was leading me into a lifetime of pastoral ministry. That night in our cabin, when the students were reflecting on their experiences, I began to share mine. I'll never forget, even at a young age, when one of the boys in our group said, "Oh, you just feel that way 'cause your parents are in the ministry." I lingered with that thought, *Lord, am I going in the ministry just because my parents are ministers? Am I doing this as a default? Am I going into this because it's everybody else's assumption?*

God wonderfully confirmed His calling during my sophomore year at Central Bible College during a spiritual emphasis week. Denny Duron spoke about "fourth-quarter Christianity," and he talked about chasing after the dreams and the plans that God has placed in our lives. When I went to the altar, I had a Bethel moment. Just as clearly as Jacob could identify the stone on which he slept when he had his vision of God, I could take you back to the place in that chapel where I really met God. I felt Him impress upon my heart, "I am calling you not because your parents were in the ministry, not because it's other peoples' expectation, but because I want to use you."

That's when Ephesians 2:10 (NLT) became very clear to me. Paul said, "For we are God's masterpiece. He has created us anew in Christ Jesus." But I love the second part of this verse that just resonates with me: "So we can do the good things he planned for us long ago." At that moment, at that Bible college altar, I became convinced. The Holy Spirit solidified in me that God has some good deeds that are unique to me. They are not my parents' deeds. They are not my brother or my sister's deeds, but they are very unique to me. And so on this ministry journey, even this assignment as general superintendent, I accept as part of those good deeds that God had prepared in advance for me to do.

Please join me in praying for the next generation to have two very unique Pentecostal experiences in the Assemblies of God: May they encounter the baptism in the Holy Spirit, and may they have multiple key opportunities to hear the voice of the Lord as it relates to their own personal calling and what He wants them to do.

CHURCH LIFE

I'm a product of the local church. I believe in the church. I'm what some people would call a church health enthusiast. All the major life-impacting events in my life happened in the church. I was dedicated as a baby in the church. I got saved in the church. I was baptized in the Holy Spirit in the church. I received my call into ministry in the church. I was married in the church. I love this thing called the church.

As one pastor says, and I believe it with all my heart, the church really is the hope of America. And, yet, the church has been impacted by rapid, radical changes within our culture that have left too many churches teetering between ineffectiveness and even extinction.

Every church has a driving force. It might be driven by tradition or finance or a key ministry personality, program, or event. Some churches are driven by the constant upkeep and expansion of a building. But what *should* drive the church? What on earth is the church supposed to be doing and why?

When the Church, with a capital C, was born in Acts 2, it centered around Christ. Jesus was the central focus. The form, the function, the focus, even the fellowship of the Jerusalem church were all centered around Jesus. That was Acts 2. As the church expanded to Greece, elements within it became philosophical. When much of the church was centralized in Rome, it became institutional. Over the centuries, as the church expanded across the globe, it absorbed countless cultural expressions. As wonderful a component as the church has been in America's history, I think you can agree with me that at times it has become sort of a business enterprise.

I'm all in *for* the church. I love the church. But I am concerned about some challenges facing the church during this unique time in history. I believe the church is struggling with an identity crisis. As just one example, think of the corporate labels we attach to a church. Are you a megachurch? Are you an emerging church? Are you a seeker-sensitive church? Are you a classical Pentecostal church? Are you a community-minded church?

The church was never intended to be a business with a cross on its roof, tweaked by a bunch of professionals. First and foremost, we must remember the church's identity as Christ's body. "Now you are the body of Christ, and each one of you is a part of it" (1 Corinthians 12:27). When we forget our central identity and purpose, we easily fall prey to critical evaluation: *The church is the only place that shoots its wounded. The church doesn't meet my needs. The church is too shallow. The church is too irrelevant.*

Whenever we lose sight of our central identity as the body of Christ, we can be swayed by society's varied expectations. *The church has no business being in politics. The church should take more of a stand on certain issues. The church needs to be more practical.* Listen, to what Jesus said about the church in Matthew 16:18 (ESV): "And I tell you, you are Peter, and on this rock, I will build my church, and the gates of hell will not prevail against it." Notice those five words: "*I* will build my church."

This verse takes me to my second point: Christ has ownership of and authority over the church. The church is Christ's creation. He made that clear from the very beginning. He's the architect, He's the originator. He protects, He leads. He's the Head. We in church or pastoral leadership are not the key to success—although we can mess it up—but *He* is. I think it's important for every pastor to ask if Jesus is the Head of the church where they serve.

Third, I believe the church will survive, because Jesus said the gates of hell will not prevail against it. The church always has overcome odds, from the Early Church in the Upper Room to the Corinthian church, where the message of the Cross seemed to be contrary to prevailing cultural ideas.

So, I have great hope for a thriving church in the twenty-first century, as long as we keep Jesus at the center and we follow the biblical blueprint for what a healthy church should look like. There should be authentic worship. There should be genuine love for one another. There should be consistent teaching. And there should be intentional equipping.

I'm passionate about the church because of its personal contribution to my life, and because I believe that a healthy church in a community provides such great hope. As a result of my deep love for the church, I am passionate about church planting and church revitalization.

Church planting through the Assemblies of God is done through the Church Multiplication Network. CMN is the official church planting arm of the Assemblies of God U.S.A. We are deeply dedicated to planting healthy, Spirit-empowered churches in every community in the United States. To do this, we must work strategically to equip, to fund, and to network new faith communities. I'm happy to report that the Church Multiplication Network of the Assemblies of God is excelling and doing well.

I am also aware of the reality that some of our churches are struggling or have plateaued. But I have great news for this need. We have a proven strategy for injecting new life and growth into plateaued and struggling churches. It's called the Acts 2 Journey.

The Acts 2 Journey is a ministry dedicated to helping churches fulfill their God-given purpose. It's a transformative process led by Spirit-empowered, seasoned leaders and ministers to help a struggling church regain momentum. It's based right out of Scripture, and the unwavering mission is to help every church become an Acts 2 church, built on this model: connect, grow, serve, go, worship. The Acts 2 Journey is not a cookie-cutter approach to church health. Every church is different in context, size, location, culture, personality, strengths, and weaknesses, but there are some common needs all churches have and some biblical principles that can restore a church's effectiveness.

CMN and the Acts 2 Journey are two proven ways for the church planting and church revitalization that I believe are going to transform the Assemblies of God in days to come.

The church? I'm all-in. I love the local church. I want to pass on to the next generation a healthy church that is fulfilling its biblical purposes. I don't want to hand off to the next generation a church that's ineffective, irrelevant, or torn away from its Pentecostal roots.

Thank you, pastor; thank you, church board member; thank you, Sunday School teacher, Royal Rangers leader, or church volunteer. May all of us give renewed attention to our local church and give ourselves to seeing our local church reach its redeemed potential. God's church is not some religious social club or fraternity. The church is God's primary instrument for reaching the world—so the effectiveness of the local church matters!

MISSIONS
God's Heart, God's Supply

Like so many across our Fellowship, I am committed to personally participating in missions and representing this Fellowship as a strong missions Movement. That commitment has nothing to do with denominational obligation. I've never supported a missionary or a ministry because of a position I have held. When I was a district youth director, my support of Speed the Light was not out of obligation to that position.

When I came to our national offices years ago, my continued support for Assemblies of God World Missions had no connection with my proximity to AGWM's administration. At every turn throughout my life, supporting missions has been integral to who I am as a follower of Christ. Missions is the DNA of this Fellowship. Missions has powerfully shaped my own personal experience in following Christ. And, most important of all, participating in missions is a fundamental biblical command.

A bedrock concept of Assemblies of God missions philosophy has never changed, and it still works: the indigenous church. AGWM missionaries and ministries address a lot of causes; but opening churches, building Bible schools, and training believers for ministry is really our sweet spot in missions. The staggering growth of the Assemblies of God worldwide has a direct correlation with the

Assemblies of God U.S.A. believing that opening churches, building Bible schools, and training nationals is our missional priority.

A lot of pastors today seem to be rediscovering missions. In fact, being "missional" is a popular buzzword. I would submit to you that being missional goes beyond missiological thinking. It's missiological *action*. It's letting God shape our view of missions, and recognizing missions as integral to the healthy spiritual life of every believer and every church.

We naturally consider missions from the classic Great Commission verses. "All authority has been given to Me in heaven and on earth. Go therefore and make disciples of all the nations" (Matthew 28:18–19, NASB). "Go into all the world and preach the gospel to all creation" (Mark 16:15, NASB). "As the Father has sent Me, I also send you," (John 20:21, NASB). In my own times of prayer and Scripture study, I have been challenged to consider our missions mandate from another foundational fact—that all of us are made in the image of God (Genesis 1:26). That image of God has been stamped on everyone.

The image of God refers to the immaterial part of people that enables them to talk with God. It's the mental, the moral, the social likeness. Think about it: God has endowed us with an intellect so we have the ability to choose. We have the ability to reason. We have the ability to grow in knowledge. We have a moral aptitude. Humans are the only one of God's creatures that has a spirit, or a God-consciousness. Our greatest and most distinctive quality as humans is our capacity for knowing God. All people have this ability to know their Creator; therefore, we have an obligation to help everyone taste and see that the Lord is good.

There's a social likeness. People were created for fellowship, and this is reflected in the Trinity. God, who is love, created humans with this social nature and need for love. You say, "Well, Doug, what's your point?" Society and culture have twisted and mangled the truth that the image of God resides in all of us. But it does, and since the image of God resides in all people, then all people matter to God. All people have the ability to respond to God, and all people can fulfill their God-given potential. But to do any of those things, all people must be correctly introduced to God.

Missions breathes life into our churches. The first church I pastored following my years with National Youth Ministries was Calvary Assembly in Toledo, Ohio. Calvary had experienced a series of tragedies and had been deeply hurt by the way in which several pastors had left the church. It was a wounded church. It was a church deep in debt. It was a divided church. It was a church that was struggling to regain trust in the office of the pastor.

When I arrived at Calvary, it was under district supervision. Only a few hundred people were left. But, despite every difficulty, the church had sustained its commitment to missions. During each of the negative transitions of pastors, they never once missed their missions commitment to their missionaries. Even when it seemed the doors of that church might be closed, Calvary's strong commitment to missions—the congregants' shared belief that expanding the kingdom of God was bigger than any of their own challenges—never wavered.

Missions is about participating in what God is doing around the world. Because Calvary recognized their responsibility to God, their doors remained open. Today, that church is several thousand strong. It's a life-giving church. They are engaged at several levels of missions, and I believe it was the high value they placed on missions that stabilized them during a time of transition.

I have witnessed this truth up close and personal. My mom is in her mid-eighties. She is widowed. She is still involved in the work of the Lord. Recently, I was concerned about her financial security and wanted to make sure she was taken care of. She is in good health and will probably continue to live a good number of years. I wanted to be sure she was being provided for. I asked Mom to send me her tax returns. She agreed.

When I looked over her records, there were no initial surprises. Her annual income from Social Security, supplemented by modest interest from a retirement fund, came out to the tune of $27,500. But then I noticed her charitable giving— Mom had literally given more than $19,000 to missions. I called her. "Mom," I said, in some alarm, "you gotta throttle that back. Mom, how can you possibly . . ." She interrupted me. "Honey, honey, honey," she said with complete calm, "you can't outgive God." And you know? She's right. All these years, my mom has had a commitment to missions, and God has provided for her.

I also believe missions has the ability to clarify the identity of what it means to be Assemblies of God. We have passed our first century as a Fellowship, and Assemblies of God churches today look quite different than they did even a few years ago. The growing diversity of our Fellowship is a beautiful thing to behold, but if we're not careful, it can ultimately lead to a lessening of or a diluting of missions philosophy and in support. There's always a struggle between projects and boots on the ground, a struggle between the local and the global, the growth of the national church having the ability to connect with some of our pastors locally. All these wonderful growth pains, if we're not careful, can put a strain on the indigenous church and the boots on the ground philosophy.

I believe that when Assemblies of God churches rally around Pentecost and missions, those commitments act as unifying forces. Pentecost and missions commitment work together to clarify our Assemblies of God identity regardless of our church's worship style, our ministry expression, or the people groups our particular church is trying to reach. Maybe you're urban. Maybe you're suburban. Maybe you're classical Pentecostal or more contemporary Pentecostal. Our commitment to missions is what I believe is our bedrock for today's stability and tomorrow's growth. I have a cause, and I have a passion to see that Assemblies of God ministers and churches fully engage in missions. That's who we've been raised up by the Spirit to be.

Why do I give to missions personally? I started my involvement in giving to missions in high school through Speed the Light, and I have not stopped giving since. I have attempted to increase that giving every year. The fact of the matter is, as Mom so pointedly reminded me, you just can't outgive God. But why? Why do I personally give, and why do I want this Fellowship to be all-in when it comes to missions?

Well, first, because our responsibility is to make disciples of all nations and all ethnicities, not just in the United States. Second, the business of the Great Commission is to get people ready. It's not only to get people ready *for* heaven, but it's to get people *into* heaven. Third, I personally participate in missions because money talks, and I want to proclaim the glory of God. You look at our culture, and I've seen money do bad things. I've seen money break up marriages, destroy family values. It supports industries that just wreak havoc in peoples' lives. But I want to use it to bring people to a saving knowledge of Jesus Christ.

I also participate in giving and praying and believing in missions because time doesn't wait, and I want to respond with my best right now. So it is my prayer that every Assemblies of God church would have, as an integral part of its character, its personal participation in missions.

LEADERSHIP PRINCIPLES
from Jesus' Life

Jesus practiced servant leadership better than anyone. To me, there is no greater demonstration of His commitment to service than when He, the King of kings, was willing to wash the feet of His followers (see John 13:1–17). There are many ways to "wash the feet" of those you lead. It can be something as fundamental as feeling equally or more excited when someone else on your team succeeds than when you are complimented for a job well done. It's not having to talk so much about yourself, but inviting others to talk about themselves. It's having others feel better about themselves when they are around you.

Jesus was willing to invest in people others would have dismissed. Consider the first time Jesus met Simon Peter. In John 1, after they were introduced, Jesus said to Simon, "I'm going to call you Peter." Simon means "small"; Peter means "rock." The Lord was saying, "Peter, you're the kind of person I want to build My church on." Changing that apostle's name from "small" to "rock," Jesus raised Peter's confidence and began building a servant who would become a world changer.

It blows my mind to contemplate Jesus as all-knowing and how that divine knowledge interacts with His love for and relationship with each of us. Jesus knew Peter would deny Him. But Jesus saw

Peter from day one for who Peter could be, not just who he was in that moment. It was as if the Lord saw Peter preaching on the Day of Pentecost, and operated on that vision rather than on the basis of Peter denying Him.

Jesus modeled trusteeship rather than ownership in His leadership. People who lead with this mind-set regard themselves as trustees of their positions for the good of their respective circles of influence, rather than as owners for their own real or symbolic benefit. Regardless of the externals of our positions, as followers of Christ, we are all stewards of the gospel and our calling to connect the lost with that good news and point them to the Savior.

Jesus exercised leadership over life's circumstances. He took what others might perceive as distractions or interruptions and recognized divine appointments. When the woman who had been bleeding for twelve years touched His garment, Jesus stopped to heal her, even though He was headed elsewhere (Mark 5:25–34). Interruptions can lead to divine appointments.

Jesus fed His own spiritual well-being, recognizing that He had to remain in touch with His Father if He was to carry out His Father's plans for ministering to others. Jesus constantly slipped away to spend time with God. I carry a deep burden for the spiritual well-being of our ministers. I was recently talking to a minister who is in our restoration program, and asked him how he was doing. He replied, "I've never felt this healthy spiritually!" Although I was excited for him and was encouraged by his comment, I asked myself why he couldn't feel spiritually healthy while in the ministry.

Finally, Jesus finished well, and He had a succession plan. Any questions whether His ministry was effective? It is still at work today in the worldwide body of Christ. The key to that continuity was Jesus' ability to lead even as He was planning to transfer that leadership to others in order to propel His ministry forward. He told the disciples He would not always be with them, but that through the power of the Holy Spirit they could function as His successors (John 16:5–15).

If servant leadership is the umbrella description of Jesus' leadership style, it is also valuable to look at key character traits Jesus lived out to perfection as our model God-follower.

Jesus maintained healthy *spirituality*. His heart belonged completely to His Father. "The eyes of the LORD move to and fro throughout the earth that He may strongly support those whose heart is completely His" (2 Chronicles 16:9, NASB). That is the essence of spirituality, complete identification with our Heavenly Father.

Integrity is better defined by actions than just words. As it relates to spiritual leadership, integrity is not so much something we do, as it is who we are. Integrity is all about personal wholeness versus fragmentation. Integrity doesn't involve divided loyalties or interests. Integrity doesn't allow our lips to violate our hearts. Integrity doesn't allow popularity to override principle. Integrity doesn't break promises that are made. Integrity doesn't mean perfection, but it does mean consecration.

Jesus is our model for spirituality. He is our model for integrity.

And, at every point in His life, He is our model for *humility*. It requires unflagging diligence to walk in spiritual confidence while simultaneously nurturing a humble heart. Yet, humility is a spiritual discipline that, when practiced, guarantees that God will show up in a powerful way. "If my people, who are called by my name, will humble themselves and pray and seek my face and turn from their wicked ways, then I will hear from heaven and I will forgive their sin and will heal their land" (2 Chronicles 7:14). What a promise! I also return regularly to Psalm 25:9: "He guides the humble in what is right and teaches them his way."

Why is Christlike character important? Making Jesus' character your own will impact your ministry in three key ways.

You need character for the sake of your *reputation*. Ministries that are respected are led by ministers who can be trusted.

1 Timothy 3:7

"He must also have a good reputation with outsiders, so that he will not fall into disgrace and into the devil's trap." Nothing will ruin your reputation faster, and more permanently, than a breach of ethical integrity.

Proverbs 22:1 (NLT)

"Choose a good reputation over great riches; being held in high esteem is better than silver or gold."

Proverbs 22:1 (GNT)

"If you have to choose between a good reputation and great wealth, choose a good reputation."

You need Jesus' character for the sake of your own *character*. If it is important to keep a good reputation, it's a thousand times more important to safeguard your personal character. A corrupt character spoils your reputation.

Matthew 7:15 (NLT)

"Beware of false prophets who come disguised as harmless sheep but are really vicious wolves."

Matthew 7:18 (NLT)

"A good tree can't produce bad fruit, and a bad tree can't produce good fruit."

You need to demonstrate Jesus' character for the sake of your *testimony*. Your reputation is what people say about you; your testimony is what your character, your behavior, and your words say about God.

What's communicated when a minister lacks ethical integrity? That person is saying that they don't really believe things like:

Proverbs 21:3 (NLT)

"The LORD is more pleased when we do what is right and just than when we offer him sacrifices."

Proverbs 15:8 (KJV)

"The sacrifice of the wicked is an abomination to the LORD: but the prayer of the upright is his delight."

Psalm 51:6 (NLT)

"But you desire honesty from the womb, teaching me wisdom even there."

Jesus' integrity was unimpeachable. Billy Graham once said, "Integrity is the glue that holds our way of life together. We must constantly strive to keep our integrity intact. When wealth is lost, nothing is lost; when health is lost, something is lost; when character is lost, all is lost."

SACRED SEXUALITY

We're living in a time when our culture seeks to redefine human sexuality, particularly as it relates to the value of life, the purpose of sex, and the sanctity of marriage. The Bible affirms human sexuality as part of God's original creation—something He considered to be beautiful and good, like everything else He made. But in our culture today, human sexuality is being twisted, perverted, and reduced to a marketing ploy.

I believe that, as the body of Christ, we are to defend key sacred values relating to human sexuality.

First of all, Christ's followers recognize the immeasurable value of life. Scripture is very clear that God has a purpose for every unborn child. The Bible says that God planned our lives even before we were born. "You saw me before I was born. Every day of my life was recorded in your book. Every moment was laid out before a single day had passed" (Psalm 139:16, NLT). Another version says, "Your eyes saw my unformed substance; in your book were written, every one of them, the days that were formed for me, when as yet there was none of them."

I am convinced there is no such thing as an accidental baby. There may be accidental parents, but there is no such thing as an illegitimate child. People apply that label—often with very destructive results in a child's life—but God is bigger than any human mistake, and He has a wonderful, life-shaping plan for every child who comes into this world.

Unfortunately, the concept of the value of life is approached from different perspectives. It gets approached from the political perspective; it gets approached from the women's rights perspective. But I submit that the only true perspective is a biblical perspective. Psalm 139:13–15 (NLT), leading up to the verse we just considered, gives deep insight into God's view of, and ultimate involvement with, each of our lives: "You made all the delicate, inner parts of my body and knit me together in my mother's womb. Thank you for making me so wonderfully complex! Your workmanship is marvelous—how well I know it. You watched me as I was being formed in utter seclusion, as I was woven together in the dark of the womb."

I heard one pastor say, "If the unborn child is not a living person, then there's no excuse necessary for abortion. But if the unborn child is a living person, then no excuse for abortion is acceptable." We must teach our children at an early age the value of life—how God sees each of our lives and how God declares each of us to be precious in His sight.

A second area of human sexuality that the body of Christ must define and defend is the purpose of sex itself. Not only do I believe life is sacred and conception is sacred, I believe that sex is sacred. Why? Because God created sex. He designed sex to be enjoyed in the context of marriage, and the only positive portrayals of human sexuality in Scripture are within that context. As just one example, consider Hebrews 13:4: "Marriage should be honored by all, and the marriage bed kept pure."

Sex is viewed as anything but sacred in our God-denying culture. Repeatedly, our society reduces sex to a ploy for the entertainment industry, to an advertising gimmick for the media world, and to an amoral academic subject for the educational system. Call it what you want—casual, recreational, protected, consensual—the fact remains, our bodies were never designed or created or intended to have sexual relations outside of marriage.

We must teach our children, at an early age, a good, healthy, biblical view of human sexuality—God's plan for it. I want God's Word, not television or any other media outlet, to shape my grandchildren's understanding of sex.

The sanctity of marriage is the third value we must define and defend regarding human sexuality. Again, the Bible is clear about God's view of marriage—one man, one woman, for life. God's intended original design has never changed. He even created our body parts to fit together with a clear purpose. "Haven't you read," Jesus said in Matthew 19:4–6, "that at the beginning the Creator 'made them male and female,' and said, 'For this reason a man will leave his father and mother and be united to his wife, and the two will become one flesh'? So they are no longer two, but one flesh. Therefore what God has joined together, let no one separate."

When it comes to the sanctity of marriage, the Bible's stance is non-negotiable. You either can accept it or you can reject it. It's not a conservative or a liberal thing, it's a scriptural thing. Now let's be honest. The message of the Cross and the message of biblical morality have always been contrary to culture. That was evidenced even in the church in Corinth. There was a tension between God's plan for human sexuality as expressed through the message of the Cross and the libertine sexual practices in Corinth as promoted by various idolatrous creeds. Our American culture's messages regarding sexuality are just as far removed from the gospel's messages as Corinth's were.

Sadly, even within the churches of America, human sexuality is being defined and lived out contrary to God's plan. I'm convinced this refusal to live within His guidelines in this area has created more problems than any other sin.

So, how should the believer, and our Assemblies of God fellowship of believers, respond? How can we reassert the value of life, the purpose of sex, and the sanctity of marriage?

Number one, we must unconditionally accept God's Word as our final authority. His Word is the only source that won't lie to us.

Second, we must always keep our words and our actions seasoned with the spirit of Jesus. As I noted above, labeling a child as "illegitimate" will never encourage God's work of grace in that life. In a similar manner, anytime Christ's followers resort to name-calling or harassment or hatred, the spread of the gospel is compromised.

Third, it is absolutely essential that we stay in love with people—especially those people who are trapped within lifestyles and choices we know to be eternally destructive. And the biblical concept of love always goes beyond mere words to include concrete action. We must never forget that it is by grace that we are saved through faith, not of ourselves, but as a gift of God.

Yes, we live in a time of widespread sexual promiscuity and a growing social acceptance of adultery, homosexuality, the use of pornography, and a host of other ungodly sexual practices. Our world today looks a lot like the world of the Bible. Like our American culture, the Greek and Roman cultures embraced sexual excess. May we approach these matters as the apostles did, by calling people to put aside the deeds of darkness (Romans 13:12–14), to avoid judging others (Romans 14:10), and to acknowledge our own sin, but in the context of God's grace (Romans 7:15–25).

PRAYER PRIORITIES

The history of the General Council of the Assemblies of God in the United States is a remarkable story of ordinary people who did extraordinary things in the power of the Spirit. Who would have ever imagined that from the first General Council, held April 1914, with about three hundred ministers and delegates, that today the worldwide Assemblies of God family would number over sixty-eight million adherents gathering in more than 370,000 churches?

As the thirteenth general superintendent of this great Fellowship, I am overwhelmed by this assignment. I understand the need to steward this sacred Movement, not in my own strength, but by embracing the words the Lord said to Zechariah: "Not by might, nor by power, but by my Spirit, says the LORD of hosts" (Zechariah 4:6, ESV). I am praying daily for wisdom, discernment, and anointing.

When I study the heritage of this Movement, it is very clear that it was born of the power of the Holy Spirit. But it is also clear that the Spirit was moving through the hard work, determination, and great sacrifice of leaders who have advanced this church. It reminds me of Hezekiah, who Scripture says worked diligently to repair the walls that protected them from an invading Assyrian army and yet declared, "We have the Lord our God to help us."

Hard work and divine assistance. Spirit and strategy. As I accept this assignment, I ask that people across this Fellowship join me in praying for three powerful blessings from the Lord—not only in my life, but in the lives of all who would carry out the Lord's purposes for the Assemblies of God.

First, we need wisdom, or supernatural judgment. King Solomon's greatest strength as a leader was wisdom. In fact, when given the opportunity to ask for anything from God for his leadership assignment, he asked for wisdom. God was so pleased with his request that He granted Solomon incredible wisdom, and much more—including discernment.

"So give your servant a discerning heart to govern your people and to distinguish between right and wrong. For who is able to govern this great people of yours?"

The Lord was pleased that Solomon had asked for this. So God said to him, "Since you have asked for this and not for long life or wealth for yourself, nor have asked for the death of your enemies but for discernment in administering justice, I will do what you have asked. I will give you a wise and discerning heart, so that there will never have been anyone like you, nor will there ever be. Moreover, I will give you what you have not asked for—both wealth and honor—so that in your lifetime you will have no equal among kings. And if you walk in obedience to me and keep my decrees and commands as David your father did, I will give you a long life." (1 Kings 3:9–14)

I desperately want the tenure of this administration to be marked by the wisdom of God. The wisdom of God starts with the fear of God.

Fear of the LORD is the foundation of true knowledge, but fools despise wisdom and discipline. (Proverbs 1:7, NLT)

And wisdom that begins with the fear of the Lord will always attract the favor of the Lord!

Like every one of my predecessors who has served in this office, I want more than anything to see the favor of the Lord continue to rest on the Assemblies of God. I have no doubt that God will continue to demonstrate His favor on this Fellowship for as long as we allow the wisdom of God to lead us.

The Assemblies of God has a solid history of promoting education across the United States and around the world. Our colleges and universities in the United States are training thousands of gifted men and women to take their places of leadership in our churches and in countless other career paths God has designed for them. I'm grateful for every instructor who invested in me at Central Bible College. I readily agree that learning can make a person knowledgeable. But here is a key truth: Only God can make a person wise! Like Paul, our leadership team's prayer will be:

> *Asking God, the glorious Father of our Lord Jesus Christ, to give you spiritual wisdom and insight so that you might grow in your knowledge of God. I pray that your hearts will be flooded with light so that you can understand the confident hope he has given to those he called—his holy people who are his rich and glorious inheritance. (Ephesians 1:17–18, NLT)*

Second, we need discernment, or supernatural insight. Discernment goes hand in hand with wisdom. I describe discernment as that ability to comprehend what is obscure and to go beyond the obvious; discernment allows us to excavate deeper into an issue than surface knowledge, or even long-tried wisdom. It is a spiritual perception of what is occurring that is not obvious or evident to the natural eye.

Unfortunately, some people limit the meaning of discernment to just a God-given awareness between good and evil, or a distinction of truth and lies. Although discernment does mean this, godly discernment is also having the understanding and insight into a situation that is not necessarily about what is right or wrong, but can clearly identify what is best. I am praying for that expression of discernment in my life.

Discernment is critical for spiritual leadership! Without it leaders stumble, they get tripped up, they impulsively make decisions based on experience. My prayer and the prayer of our leadership team will be:

My son, pay attention to my wisdom; listen carefully to my wise counsel. Then you will show discernment, and your lips will express what you've learned. (Proverbs 5:1–2)

Third, we need anointing, or supernatural assistance. On October 31, 1517, Martin Luther staged one of the most important protests in history. Roman Catholic officials were promising people forgiveness in exchange for money. Luther nailed a long list of challenges on the door of a church in Wittenberg, Germany.

Luther's famous ninety-five theses spread like wildfire. Like Jeremiah, Luther dared to ask questions that had never been asked. Through Luther, the Holy Spirit sparked the Protestant Reformation and restored the doctrine of grace to a church that had become corrupt, falsely religious, dysfunctional, and spiritually dead.

I'm no Luther, but I firmly believe we need a Pentecostal Reformation. If I could nail a list of critical values on the door of every Assemblies of God church, I would start with four principles.

First, as Pentecostals, we must never forget that the Holy Spirit is a Person, not an it. He is the third Person of the Trinity, He is God, and He is holy. We ignore Him to our peril. We demonstrate shocking hubris when we try to manipulate or command Him. Yet, if we will acknowledge, honor, and respect Him, He will do what He does best—magnify Jesus!

Second, as people of the Word, we must never lose sight of the Bible as truth, absolute truth. God's Word

is not just a piece of literature. Some would treat this Book as a classic filled with nice sayings suitable for sympathy cards or graduation announcements. The Bible is the foundation for all we believe and the whole Christian experience. It is the primary tool we should rely on for discerning spirits and keeping deception from spreading.

Third, as a holy people, we must demonstrate in word and deed that character matters—regardless of our title. From those who operate in the prophetic or have the gift of healing, don't ever promote your gifts at the expense of character. I don't care if you can fill a stadium or write a best-selling book—if the fruit of the Spirit is not exhibited or seen in your life, then you are an out-of-tune instrument (1 Corinthians 13).

Fourth, as people on a God-given mission, we cannot become sidetracked from our purpose. In 1914, at one of the first organized conventions of the Assemblies of God, the delegates and ministers adopted this resolution, a vision statement: "We commit ourselves and the Movement to Him for the greatest evangelism the world has ever seen." As I serve fellow ministers and our laity, I pray that every one of us will stay the course. May we always discern the Spirit's leading over every trend or well-marketed church campaign.

I pray we would remain immersed in those things that are the sweet spot of this Fellowship—evangelism, church planting, missions, compassion ministries. Those priorities have given us a wonderful history for more than a century. Maintaining those values will continue to make us missionally fruitful in the twenty-first century.

We are living in unique times. We are called to minister to a fractured world, a world that can never be fixed through economic reform, attempts at world peace, or the buildup of military strength. This fracture cannot be fixed by monetary and earthly things because the fracture is spiritual in nature and the result of humanity's alienation from God.

Only Jesus can heal our fractured world. We are called to proclaim Him as that Healer, as well as Savior, Baptizer, and Soon-Coming King. I am that convinced, there has never been a finer hour for the Assemblies of God, or for the Church as a whole, to step forward with that proclamation and with a personal demonstration of His transforming grace already at work in our lives.

PLEASE PRAY!

Doug has requested prayer for three things:
wisdom—supernatural judgment
discernment—supernatural insight
anointing—supernatural assistance
We ask you to make a note on your calendar, one day each month, to pray for these three requests for Doug, as well as for the other members of the Executive Leadership Team at the national office of the Assemblies of God:

Doug Clay, general superintendent
Alton Garrison, assistant general superintendent
Rick Dubose, general treasurer
James T. Bradford, general secretary
Gregory M. Mundis, executive director of World Missions
Malcolm Burleigh, executive director of US Missions

With all prayer and petition pray at all
times in the Spirit, and with this in view,
be on the alert with all perseverance
and petition for all the saints.

Ephesians 6:18 (NASB)